Falling Deeply Into America

Falling Deeply Into America

Poems by

Gregory Djanikian

Carnegie Mellon University Press
Pittsburgh 2011

Acknowledgments

Grateful acknowledgement is made to the editors of the following magazines in which these poems first appeared:

The American Scholar: "My Aunt Gives Me A Clarinet Lesson"

Cimarron Review: "The Fight," "For My Daughter"

Iowa Review: "Agami Beach," "Great-Grandfather's Nurse," "Mme. Sperides," "Beethoven: Sonata No. 14," "Gathering Hay," "Correspondence"

New England Review: "Where He Is, I Am"

Poetry: "Grandmother's Rugs," "When I First Saw Snow," "In the Elementary School Choir," "How I Learned English," "Clouds," "These Are the Gifts," "The Theft," "Alexandria, 1953," "The Boy Who Had Eleven Toes," "Late At Night In Bed"

Three Rivers Poetry Journal: "The Boy in the Mirror," " 'You Can't Tell One Assassin From Another' "

Yankee: "The City Garden," "Movie Extras"

* * *

"Mme. Sperides" has been anthologized in the *Annual Survey of American Poetry: 1986*.

"How I Learned English," "In The Elementary School Choir," and "When I First Saw Snow" were awarded the Eunice Tietjens Memorial Prize from *Poetry*.

* * *

I would like to thank the National Endowment for the Arts for a writing fellowship which enabled me to complete this book.

Library of Congress Control Number 2011920378
ISBN 978-0-88748-542-8

Printed and bound in the United States of America

10 9 8 7 6 5 4 3 2 1

First Carnegie Mellon University Press Classic Contemporaries Edition, May 2011

Falling Deeply Into America was first published by Carnegie Mellon University Press in 1989.

Contents

I

II

III

For Ariel, Zachary and Jill

I

Alexandria, 1953

You could think of sunlight
Glancing off the minarets,
You could think of guavas and figs
And the whole marketplace filled
With the sumptuous din of haggling,
But you could not think of Alexandria
Without the sea, or the sea,
Turquoise and shimmering, without
The white city rising before it.

Even on the back streets
You could feel it on your skin,
You could smell it in the aroma
Of dark coffee, spiced meat.

You looked at the sea and you heard
The wail of an Arab woman singing or praying.

If, as I can now, you could point
To the North Atlantic, swollen
And dark as it often is, you might say,
"Here lies Wrath," or "Truly God is great."
You could season a Puritan soul by it.

But you could fall into the Mediterranean
As though you were falling into a blue dream,
Gauzy, half unreal for its loveliness.
It was deceptively calm and luxurious.
At Stanley Bay, you could float
On your back and watch the evening sun
Color the city a faint rose.
You could drown, it was said,
Almost without knowing it.

Agami Beach
Alexandria, 1955

There were the black flags flying
All along the beach and we knew
We could not swim. There was the sea
Turning too dark and churlish
And there was someone wading in
Too far and standing for a moment
Half in air, half in water.
There was the sand shifting easily
Under his heels and the current
Sweeping him out and out.
There were the cabanas and the sound
Of my sister crying and my feet
Were burning as I ran toward them
But there was my father moving already
Rope in hand sprinting to the water's
Edge and plunging into the sea.
There was my sister crying
"Don't let him go, don't let him die"
And I grew angry at feeling
Her fear, hearing those words.
There was the long line of watchers
And my father's head weaving
In and out of the waves, his arm
Around the other, a speck of light
In the darkness. There was the fear
I shook off as my father
Shook off the sea emerging,
Dragging the body along the hot white sand.
There was the skin blue like water,
There were fingernails the color of plums.
There was my father standing above it
Spent and awkward and full of mercy.
There were the people running toward it

From all directions and there was someone
Pulling us away and my sister crying
"Take it back, take it back!"
It was getting dark. The sea-birds
Were calling to one another, diving,
And no one was moving.

Years later,
My sister would suddenly say:
"The colors were all wrong.
I remember the day by its colors."
We were sitting at a table
All afternoon drinking wine
And calling up one name after another
Of friends we had almost forgotten.
Mourad, Nadia, where were they now?
We had been telling old stories
About ourselves, our lives.
We had been laughing.
I remember the blue tablecloth.
Our empty glasses were filling with sunlight.
There was a bowl full of ripe plums.

Great-Grandfather's Nurse

Alexandria, 1954

She is sitting on the terrace, holding
My small hands. Dressed in her whites,
She is the angel I have wished to touch.
Her laughter floats and falls around me
And becomes the house I want to live in.
Again, Marta, I say, again. She pulls me up
Clicking her tongue, her smooth legs
Brushing mine, and my face nestles
Into the easy scoop of her shoulder.
I smell the scent of flowers or spices.
Again, Marta, again. Upstairs
Where I do not want to go
My great-grandfather is sleeping
Through his pain and illness
And I am lucky, falling, falling
Over the landscape of Marta's legs.
My mother smiles and locks her arm
In my father's. My grandfather is winking
And whispering into my grandmother's white hair.
Krikor, he says, you little knave,
Krikor, you scoundrel, you little mouse.
And before I know what I'm doing
I whisk the hem of her dress up,
Kiss her thigh and stand before her
Boyish and full of love.

Then what?

Confusion, shouting.
My great-grandfather waking,
Beating his cane against the metal bed.
Marta rising, climbing the stairs
Toward some retribution,

The oaths streaming down.
The terrace emptying out.
The *Allah aqbar* of the muezzin
Calling the faithful.
The minarets, the hot sun, the white city.
My lips full of fear and prayer.
My heart full of nonsense,
Never as young, and the sea,
The blue sea in the distance,
The cool, unimplicated sea.

Grandmother's Rugs

Alexandria, 1954

My father was unrolling rugs,
They were all finding their places
After a summer's storage,
The red Kashan in the hallway,
The blue prayer rug in the parlor.

My grandmother was talking.
"Vacuum cleaners," she was saying,
"They have them in America.
I've seen squirrels too. Snow.
Electric irons, the land
Is full of electricity."

The house was becoming quiet
And taking on color, my heels
Were sinking into the soft
Understory of wool.

"Rugs," she said. "In America,
The leaves in autumn turn
To the color of rugs."

I imagined the wonder of leaves
Textured like wool, the smell
Of naphthalene around every tree.

All day I walked from room to room,
From one rug to another,
"They are beautiful," my grandmother said,
"Tekkes, Baluchis, Turkistans."

But all I could think of was America,
And streets of squirrels and snow
And trees shedding color.

I walked on electric reds and purples
Thinking they were leaves,
The ceilings were a sky with bountiful light,
The windows gave way to sparks and grids of power.
"Rugs," my grandmother said.

But I was too far gone. Where was I?
Somewhere my longing had flung me,
Somewhere private and serious and new
Where there would always be,
No matter the passage of years,
A hum of wires, a crackle of leaves.

Mme. Sperides

Alexandria, 1956, after the nationalization
of the Suez Canal and all foreign capital

Perhaps her cook, come under the influence
Of a few discreet piastres, had spoken
Too indiscreetly. Or just perhaps,
On a hot day along the azure of the Mediterranean,
Rue Fouad bearing a stream of traffic
To Muhammed Ali Square in a riot
Of klaxons and shouts, and the whole city
Gleaming white as it must have from a distance,
Perhaps on such a day, someone got lucky
And Mme. Sperides at the customs house
Could sense what price she would have to pay,
That the official full of apologies
And gold teeth would usher her into
A private room smelling of dark tobacco,
That under the drone of the ceiling fans
Her valises would be searched, the linings
Cut out, the cowhide ripped back,
That despite her protests which would be
Useless but obligatory, she herself
Would be stripped, that finally,
Two large diamonds worth a modest villa
Would peek and shine from the elegant crack
Of her ass.
                    Whatever the story,
It was not for a boy to know.
I listened at my grandmother's door
As she spoke in a whisper, thieving
A fragment here a word there *naked*
Jewels   hidden you know where   though I didn't
And tried to call up all that I remembered:
Mme. Sperides in her salon serving us
Tea and the small cucumber sandwiches

Whose flavor always reminded me of paste.
Mme. Sperides falling easily back in her chair,
Crossing her legs, intoning:
"You know what my husband left me.
It is not much to live on in these times."
Mme. Sperides ringing for her servants
Who swished in and out in their galabiyas,
Expressionless, almost invisible,
Bringing us fruits and petit fours.
And now, Mme. Sperides naked, jewels hidden
Somewhere in my imagination, somewhere
In the words my grandmother whispered
And I smuggled out with my ear at the door,
Holding my breath, thinking the world
Would suddenly reveal itself with one
Prize word, some dark knowledge.
"I love you, Mme. Sperides," I tried
With a small boy's passion, believing
That was enough to bring her secretly
To me, translucent and shimmering.
But when I closed my eyes in my fever,
All I could see was Mme. Sperides laden
With rings and pearls, bracelets and brooches,
Mme. Sperides hidden by jewelry and clothing,
Something else hidden beyond all that.
All I could taste was cucumber.
All I could hear was the undercurrent
Of long robes swishing from room to room.

The Pyramids at Giza

You would take Qasr-an-Nil through Cairo
Passing Zamalik, Gesira, the tires
Sometimes hissing against the softening tar.
You would drive on the Avenue des Pyramides,
Fields of grass on either side, all the way
To the Mena House, its guest rooms
Shuttered with dark and sculpted teak.
You could see the three pyramids
From its terraced gardens, Khufu first,
A half mile away at the edge of the desert,
Surprisingly close and undesolate.

Once when I was seven, a guide, turbaned,
Dressed in a white aba, led me inside
The great pyramid through an entrance
Cut in stone. We climbed wooden stairs
Through a narrow passageway a long time
Toward the center. There were letters,
Hieroglyphs, or scrawls on the wall,
And sometimes there was the stench
Of urine, or maybe it was the smell
Of the ages, I didn't know which.
The burial chamber was empty
But for a stone slab where a sarcophagus
Might have rested, where the guide rested
Now, old and bird-like, mumbling
In Arabic something about his bad knees.
Soon we descended and came out
Into the hot sun and I remembered the story
Of Napoleon emerging here before his troops
Ashen and trembling and without words.
How do I look, I asked my father
But he was busy with the guide

Money was being exchanged, a few piastres.
We were going to go to the hotel for a soda.
There were some tourists riding camels to the Sphinx
And a woman was yelling, "Take a picture, Earl."

At the Mena House, you could always hear
A refined clinking of spoons and porcelain cups,
People dining, taking tea in the gardens.
You would drive back on the dusky roads
With this clinking in mind, Cairo a few miles off,
And you would see in the sky the amber glow
From its lights. Paris, you would think,
Budapest, Rome, it could be anywhere.
But soon you would be swallowed up
By the traffic at Isma'iliyah,
The Cairenes swelling into the streets
And the air smoky from grilled kebab and pigeon.
You would hear music, ouds plucked
And thrummed, crotals jangled, and the Nile
Flowing through the heart of the city,
And you would be in Cairo, and know it,
The desert air on your back, and the darkness
Far off but on all sides, and the now and now
Of lights and horns and shouts about you.

Photograph of my Mother

She has just gotten up from her table
In the tea room at the Hotel Cécil.
It is after el-Alamein,
After the lights in Alexandria
Have come back on and the city sparkles
And the war is a rumor drifting northward.

She is dressed in a fur coat, fur hat,
She looks Russian and aristocratic,
And her name, "Sonia," might even be on the lips
Of strangers who have turned to stare.

Behind her, young and sweet-faced,
Her husband is smiling broadly
And his eyes have the look
Of one who has managed to be lucky.

It is a time of celebrations,
Dances, who would not smile?

Never mind that in twelve years' time
She will be living in a small town
In Pennsylvania, immigrant-poor,
Her marriage about to unravel,
And her other life
A story she will tell her children
Who will blink and see stars.

Tonight at the Hotel Cécil
She is beautiful and has risen to go
And a hundred hearts in the room
Have risen with her.
Tonight moonlight is faceting the sea

And everything is possible,
A night without fire,
Love without grief,
And she, young forever,
Turning to look back, for a moment,
Without longing or want.

Sailing to America
Alexandria, 1956

The rugs had been rolled up and islands of them
Floated in the centers of every room,
And now, on the bare wood floors,
My sister and I were skimming among them
In the boats we'd made from newspaper,
Sheets of them pinned to each other,
Dhows, gondolas, clippers, arks.
There was a mule outside on the street
Braying under a load of figs, though mostly
There was quiet, a wind from the desert
Was putting the city to sleep,
But we were too far adrift, the air
Was scurfy and wet, the currents tricking
Our bows against reef and coral
And hulls shearing under the weight of cargo.
"Ahoy and belay!" I called to my sister,
"Avast, avast!" she yelled back from her rigging,
And neither of us knew what we were saying
But the words came to us as from a movie,
Cinemascopic, American. "Richard Widmark,"
I said. "Clark Gable, Bogie," she said,
"Yo-ho-ho." We had passed Cyprus
And now there was Crete or Sardinia
Maybe something larger further off.
The horizon was everywhere I turned,
The waters were becoming turgid,
They were roiling, weeks had passed.
"America, America, land-ho!" I yelled directionless.
"Gibraltar," my sister said, "Heave to,"
And signalling a right, her arm straight out,
She turned and bravely set our course
North-by-northwest for the New World.

Did we arrive? Years later, yes.
By plane, suddenly. With suitcases
And something as hazy as a future.
The November sun was pale and far off,
The air was colder than we'd ever felt,
And already these were wonders to us
As much as snow would be or evergreens,
And it would take me a long time
Before I'd ever remember
Boats made of paper, islands of wool,
And my sister's voice, as in a fog,
Calling out the hazards,
Leading me on, getting us there.

When I First Saw Snow

Tarrytown, N.Y.

Bing Crosby was singing "White Christmas"
on the radio, we were staying at my aunt's house
waiting for papers, my father was looking for a job.
We had trimmed the tree the night before,
sap had run on my fingers and for the first time
I was smelling pine wherever I went.
Anais, my cousin, was upstairs in her room
listening to Danny and the Juniors.
Haigo was playing Monopoly with Lucy, his sister,
Buzzy, the boy next door, had eyes for her
and there was a rattle of dice, a shuffling
of Boardwalk, Park Place, Marvin Gardens.
There were red bows on the Christmas tree.
It had snowed all night.
My boot buckles were clinking like small bells
as I thumped to the door and out
onto the grey planks of the porch dusted with snow.
The world was immaculate, new,
even the trees had changed color,
and when I touched the snow on the railing
I didn't know what I had touched, ice or fire.
I heard, "I'm dreaming . . ."
I heard, "At the hop, hop, hop . . . oh, baby."
I heard "B & O" and the train in my imagination
was whistling through the great plains.
And I was stepping off,
I was falling deeply into America.

In The Elementary School Choir

I had never seen a cornfield in my life,
I had never been to Oklahoma,
But I was singing as loud as anyone,
"Oh what a beautiful morning . . . . The corn
Is as high as an elephant's eye,"
Though I knew something about elephants I thought,
Coming from the same continent as they did,
And they being more like camels than anything else.

And when we sang from *Meet Me in St. Louis,*
"Clang, clang, clang went the trolley,"
I remembered the ride from Ramleh Station
In the heart of Alexandria
All the way to Roushdy where my grandmother lived,
The autos on the roadway vying
With mule carts and bicycles,
The Mediterranean half a mile off on the left,
The air smelling sharply of diesel and salt.

It was a problem which had dogged me
For a few years, this confusion of places,
And when in 5th grade geography I had pronounced
"Des Moines" as though it were a village in France,
Mr. Kephart led me to the map on the front wall,
And so I'd know where I was,
Pressed my forehead squarely against Iowa.
Des Moines, he'd said. Rhymes with coins.

Now we were singing "zippidy-doo-dah, zippidy-ay,"
And every song we'd sung had in it
Either sun or bluebirds, fair weather
Or fancy fringe, O beautiful America!
And one tier below me,

There was Linda Deemer with her amber waves
And lovely fruited plains,
And she was part of America too
Along with sun and spacious sky
Though untouchable, and as distant
As purple mountains of majesty.

"This is my country," we sang,
And a few years ago there would have been
A scent of figs in the air, mangoes,
And someone playing the oud along a clear stream.

But now it was "My country 'tis of thee"
And I sang it out with all my heart
And now with Linda Deemer in mind.
"Land where my fathers died," I bellowed,
And it was not too hard to imagine
A host of my great uncles and -grandfathers
Stunned from their graves in the Turkish interior
And finding themselves suddenly
On a rock among maize and poultry
And Squanto shaking their hands.

How could anyone not think America
Was exotic when it had Massachusetts
And the long tables of thanksgiving?
And how could it not be home
If it were the place where love first struck?

We had finished singing.
The sun was shining through large windows
On the beatified faces of all
Who had sung well and with feeling.

We were ready to file out and march back
To our room where Mr. Kephart was waiting.
Already Linda Deemer had disappeared
Into the high society of the hallway.
One day I was going to tell her something.
Des Moines, I was saying to myself,
Baton Rouge. Terre Haute. Boise.

How I Learned English

It was in an empty lot
Ringed by elms and fir and honeysuckle.
Bill Corson was pitching in his buckskin jacket,
Chuck Keller, fat even as a boy, was on first,
His t-shirt riding up over his gut,
Ron O'Neill, Jim, Dennis, were talking it up
In the field, a blue sky above them
Tipped with cirrus.
                                        And there I was,
Just off the plane and plopped in the middle
Of Williamsport, Pa. and a neighborhood game,
Unnatural and without any moves,
My notions of baseball and America
Growing fuzzier each time I whiffed.

So it was not impossible that I,
Banished to the outfield and daydreaming
Of water, or a hotel in the mountains,
Would suddenly find myself in the path
Of a ball stung by Joe Barone.
I watched it closing in
Clean and untouched, transfixed
By its easy arc before it hit
My forehead with a thud.
                                                I fell back,
Dazed, clutching my brow,
Groaning, "Oh my shin, oh my shin,"
And everybody peeled away from me
And dropped from laughter, and there we were,
All of us writhing on the ground for one reason
Or another.
                                Someone said "shin" again,
There was a wild stamping of hands on the ground,

A kicking of feet, and the fit
Of laughter overtook me too,
And that was important, as important
As Joe Barone asking me how I was
Through his tears, picking me up
And dusting me off with hands like swatters,
And though my head felt heavy,
I played on till dusk
Missing flies and pop-ups and grounders
And calling out in desperation things like
"Yours" and "take it," but doing all right,
Tugging at my cap in just the right way,
Crouching low, my feet set,
"Hum baby" sweetly on my lips.

Two Boys

When they walked up Parkwood St.
Along the rhododendrons toward his house,
They saw him through the leaves
Kissing Sandra Nieman on the mouth.
They had come to shoot marbles,
Maybe try his go-cart down Brandon Hill,
But nothing in their lives had prepared them
For what they saw, his hands fumbling
Over her shoulders and down her sides,
His glasses about to fall off,
But for all this awkwardness,
Something frightening, something inevitable,
His mouth disappearing into her mouth.
They wanted to shout and point,
"Jelly-lips," they wanted to say
Or make loud kissing noises to tease him,
To uncouple them, but they had lingered
Too long, seen too much to react
So easily, be so dismissive, so they tucked
Their cap pistols back in their pockets
And neither spoke to the other
Until they had rounded three corners
And then it was "Geez," and "Crimeny,"
Both of them shaking their heads,
Picking up stones and throwing them
At anything that stood still —
Trees, fire hydrants, stop signs —
The *pok pok pok* making them feel better, braver,
And their arms moving violently forward,
Pitching them off balance,
And beginning to ache in a way
That was immediate and familiar.

The Fight

It was over a girl,
One boy had spoken to her,
Had asked her out, the other
Had been feeling with her
The twitches of something serious.
It was a misunderstanding,
Something that might have been fixed,
Talked out or around,
But the whole school had turned out
To watch them settle it.
It was too late for talk,
It was no longer just their fight,
Something irrelevant and impure
Had entered it, honor, looking
More upright than the other,
Things which had nothing to do
With the girl, or desire,
Or what she had whispered to one of them
One night in a car.
So they faced each other,
Bringing their anger up
By saying what finally did not matter
But loudly enough so their bodies believed it.
There was a sudden coming together,
There were fists flailing
While everybody, hundreds, watched.
One was cut above the eye, the other's
Knuckles were bloodied against teeth.
It lasted half a minute until
One of them pulled back and said
Something like "This is stupid"
And the other dropped his fists
And watched him walk away

Before leaving in the other direction,
The crowd having thought the one would charge
After the other, and everybody
Looking at everybody else now, feeling
Awkward, suddenly out of place.

My Aunt Gives Me A Clarinet Lesson

"Play," my aunt said, *"pianissimo."*
I blew out toots and squeaks, filled the kitchen
With caterwauls, monkeys, pigs,
There was a menagerie, there were jungles.
"Why not the cello," she said, "why not drums."
"Zookeeper," my uncle said, "game warden."

I blew out ostriches, catbirds, snow geese.
"Silly boy," she said, creasing
The pages of the lesson book,
"Take the gum out of your mouth,
Don't blow so hard."

There were frogs at my feet,
Boat-tailed grackles perched on the towel rack.

I could hear my cousins playing ping-pong in the cellar,
There was the *tick tick* of the oven baking bread,
And wasn't that Freddy Petrie outside
Under the maple, swinging easily on a rope
And making the branch creak?

How many metronomes there were!
"Begin again," my aunt said, "restrain,"
And snapped her fingers next to my ear.
Two mules, I counted. Three cows.

Where was Benny Goodman? Dixieland?
Which house were all the saints marching in?
Farewell, Carnegie Hall, I thought. Goodbye,
Pierson Elementary School Band. So long,
Janice Reutlinger who played the tuba.

There was a yak lowing in the doorway.
"Domesticate," my aunt said, "refine."
Freddy Petrie was riding a wild donkey
Along the blackberry bushes, waving and smiling.
The maple was becoming dangerous and colorful,
Hippopotami had come.
Soon there'd be phalaropes, merinos.

"Sonority!" my aunt cried out, "Sonority!"
And ducks. There were lots of ducks.

Clouds

It was a test on clouds, Science 1,
Seventh grade, Mrs. Snyder, who,
I remember, always wore dark colors.
My fingers trembled, I couldn't keep
A point on my pencil, and in the next row,
John Carlson was getting all the answers.
Cumulus, altostratus, cirrus.

What was I dreaming of? Clouds.
They reminded me of Iowa or Kansas,
Or my notion of them, expanses of wheat,
Big skies somewhere west of where I was,
Somewhere with rural addresses, dogs
Named "Blue" or "Jake," and railroad crossings,
And a boy's river lazing through farm and pasture.

Cirrus fibratus, cirrus uncinus,
Altocumulus, cumulus congestus

I was losing time, my answer sheet
Was white as a cloud, and there was
A scratching of pencils on paper.
What was I after? Summer. A hillside.
A cumulus sky driven by the breezes.
Kites, and kite string humming in the air.
Shouts, laughter in the distance only.

Cumulus humilis, culumus fractus

Time was up and we were let go
And I reeled out to the playground lightened.
There was the bluest sky and I saw
Fibrous wisps converging into grey.
"Cirrus spissatus," John Carlson announced

From behind me, maybe to himself,
And skipped away at ease with the world.

All the way home, I spat out those names
I'd learned one by one, cirrostratus nebulosus,
Altocumulus undulatus, cirrocumulus, cumulonimbus,
Until I was left with just "cloud,"
Something vague and inexact, but prevailing,
Like some notion of happiness,
Or longings without name.

The Return

One more time I will walk
Down the streets of my boyhood,
Cherry Street, Hawthorne Avenue,
Streets of dark fruits and wild berries.
One more time I will pass
John Fedinez, Pat Molloy, going
About their business of being boys,
Richard Caldera, Harvey Kaplan,
And Miss Rosser, Miss Kelchner, waving
In their white frocks
From the grade school windows.

And already they will have gone,
Those others before me
Who have come looking.

II

The Boy in the Mirror

Wild Bill, he could outdraw himself in a mirror.
— from a story

His fingers twitch like piglets.
Under the tilt of a raccoon hat
His face has become almost cherubic.
In the rolls of his cuffs his feet disappear.
But if he seems to us a figure of fun,
Let us remember that his guns are holstered,
His eye grim, that the boy in the mirror
Has dreamt the dream of angels.
If it is possible to fire before firing,
To make the hand quicker than the eye,
Than light, he will be the first to do it.
If not, which of our rigorous explanations
Will not fall short of his longing?
His is the heresy we call faith,
And the beginning of disappointment.
Yet the boy in the mirror chides us
Hour after hour with his devotion,
Drawing, cocking the hammer, firing
The trigger, drawing, cocking, firing,
Again and again in a blur of motion
Till the sun hides its face in the sea
And evening falls to disguise the fury.
Now light speeding downward
From the farthest star catches him
Poised and aiming at his heart.
Now lamplight from the corner
Betrays him as the barrel clicks.
Each time he is faster than he was.
Each time he is only as fast as himself.
It is a test, we think ungenerously,
To marry him to failure.
Let him learn then the burden of belief.
He is not yet nine. But who can say

That by ten, he will have laid down
His clever guns, let his hands,
Empty but for the feel of something
Lost, sleep in his pockets? And who
Can say that we, too, the disenchanted
In this story of enchantments, will have turned
Our backs on the mirror, on the boy
With the quick-triggered shooters
And wrath in his hands, on our one wish
About to break free like any bullet:
Do it. Do it, boy. Do it, for us all.

Where He Is, I Am

for my son, 10 months

Zachary turns to me as I walk in,
Smiles wide and shows his six new teeth.
"Daddy," he says, but he's pointing
At the floor lamp, "Daddy," he repeats,
But at the toaster, now the fruit bowl.

My wife is coming down the stairs
In a summer dress, she is all light
And airy and Zachary loves to watch her.
"Daddy," he squeals, as she scoops him up,
And her look indicts me for ruining
His future, his sense of perception.
"Say, 'mommy,' " she says, " 'mm-o-mmm-y.' "

(Maybe I should never have whispered
So insistently in his ear, maybe
I should have kept to other words,
"Doggy," or "light bulb," or "banana.")

Now he's prowling the living room,
The kitchen, everything around him
Tumbles and is changed, building blocks,
Houseplants, sandwiches, "Daddy,"
He is saying with delight, "daddy!"

What can I do with such one-mindedness
Which puts me everywhere and nowhere?
I am embarrassingly limitless,
I am ceilings and tap water and pizzas,
I am a toy duck, there is
Nothing that means me as I am.

Now I catch him crawling out

From under the dining room table.
He has been scavenging for cereal,
Dried peas and fruit, and he thinks
His stomach is forever empty.

I pick him up high and rub
His uncovered belly with my head
And his laughter makes me
Light-hearted and spry.
"Daddy," he says, and remarkably,
His index finger is at the tip of my nose.
"Zachary," I say, pointing back,

And for a moment, we're eye to eye,
Nose to nose, and wonderfully
All of a piece, before he wriggles

Out of my hands and scurries
Into the next room, imprinting
And consuming and sending up now and then
A series of "daddy" 's above him
Burst like signal flares,
Telling me where he is,
What he's found,
What next I've become.

The Man Whom Children Love

For he will laugh easily,
Make himself as foolish as
The moment requires, become

A heifer, a steam shovel,
Seven suitcases, a calliope,
A bowling pin.

Children will often call him "Sillytunes,"
Or "Uncle Dopey," but they will hang on
To his many handles and not let go.

And even those who still shrink into doorways
And the corners of things and cry out
"Mama, mama," from their sleep

Will be swung gladly upside
Down and bonged like a bell
On their heads, again, again.

For he will dodge and howl.
He will wiggle in the fingers,
He will gallop in the knees.

Look at him on all fours! on his head!
And knick-knacks dropping from all his pockets,
Bottle caps, whistles!

Oh we are never as young
As when he visits, bringing us back
To ourselves dizzier, lighter.

Always, the door will be left ajar!

And when there is news of him coming,
Our wrinkles will dimple about our smiles,

There will be cakes and balloons
At every sitting place,
Children at every window.

For My Daughter

She has been lost in her room for hours
Singing with Alice and the Mad Hatter.
There's a forest growing out of the roof
Of her house, a hole in the bottom of the sea,
Every adventure touches on disappearance.

If I ask her what she's doing
Her eyes cloud, they look obliquely off,
"Nothing," she says, "I'm doing nothing."

How quickly she is untying herself of us!
And when she stands at her window,
The house cannot contain her
And her childhood looms above the fields
Of summer where we are forbidden.

(Perhaps, had we stood long enough
In those afternoons of light,
The wind in the shivering leaves,
Something lost and sublime might have touched us.
But there were voices calling us back.)

Let her traveling be unaccompanied, I think,
Her childhood large and digressive.
Downstairs, I try to listen to her listening,

But she suddenly throws open her door
Singing, "I'm going to Kentucky to the fair,
To see flamingos and painted flowers there,"
And comes bouncing down the stairs
Four years-old again and full of kisses.

I pull her close, I call her mine,
There's a scent of roses on her dress,
There are sprigs of wild grasses in her hair.

Schoolyard

Five girls are laughing
In blue dresses "You're it
You're it" they are touching
Each other there is a freshness
Of April crocuses trillium there is
An odor of tar something
Primeval a boy is pointing
To the daytime moon rocketing
A ball up a dark circle against
A light circle there are five
Girls laughing and a scream
A twisting of spokes a child
Falling red-cheeked red-
Toothed in winter the snow
Is waist-deep it could be
The flatlands of Kansas
Longer and who are they
In the archway smoking
Is it their breaths
In the cold there is
A clinking of knives
Or is it coins ice

Children's Hospital, Emergency Room

You do not want to be here
You wish it were you
The doctor is stitching up
It is a cut on the chin, fixable
This time but deep enough
To make you think of gashes
Puncture wounds flesh unfolding to the bone
Your child is lying on the table
Restrained, You must be still
The nurse who cradles her head is saying
And the doctor is embroidering
Delicately patiently like a kind aunt
But there is not enough solace in that
To make you stop thinking of other children
Whose hurt blooms like a dark interior bruise
In other rooms there is hysteria
The sound of glass shattering
And in the next bay there is the child
Who is sleeping too soundly
You do not want to hear such silence
The evidence which convicts, puts away
Wake up, you whisper, wake up
You want to think of water
A surface with no scars
You want the perpetuity of circles
A horizon clear and unbroken
And the sky a flat blue immensity
Without sides or depth
But there is nothing you can do
When your daughter calls out It hurts
And things regain their angularity
The vulnerable opaqueness, I'm here
You say, Be still, I'm here

Though you wish none of you were
And if anyone offered you now the life
Of the spirit you would take it for all of you
The child asleep or your child
Those in pain or mercifully out
You would take it and fly though never
Would you feel this rush of joy
As you do now when your daughter
Is returned to you unhealed but whole
Your lips pressing against her cheek
And your hands hovering
Like two shy birds about her face.

Late At Night In Bed

My wife tells me she hears a beetle
Scurrying across the kitchen floor.
She says our daughter is dreaming
Too loudly, just listen, her eyelids
Are fluttering like butterflies.

What about the thunder, I say,
What about the dispatches from the police car
Parked outside, or me rolling over like a whale?

She tells me there's a leaf falling
And grazing the downstairs window,
Or it could be glass cutters, diamonds,
Thieves working their hands toward the latch.
She tells me our son is breathing too quickly,
Is it pneumonia, is it the furnace
Suddenly pumping monoxides through the house?

So when my wife says *sleep,* she means
A closing of the eyes, a tuning
Of the ears to ultra frequencies.

(It is what always happens
When there are children, the bed
Becoming at night a listening post,
Each little *ting* forewarning disaster.)

Downstairs there is the sound
Of something brushing against something else
And I try to listen as my wife might listen,
Insects, I say, dust on a table top,
Maybe a knife's edge against the palm.

But she tells me it's only
The African violet on the windowsill
Putting out another flower,
And falls luxuriously into a dream
Of being awake and vigilant.

So the house grows noisier,
There are clicks in the woodwork,
There are drips, raps, clunks, things
To make sense of, make benign.

My son and daughter are sleeping calmly,
And the stairs, yes, are creaking,
The wind, I think, or maybe two men,
Where's the beaker of acid,
The bowling ball, the war hoop
I learned in second grade?

So this is what it's like when there's
No one left but you to love and defend.

Outside there are cats in a fight
And they remind me too much of babies crying.
Then the bottle thrown against the stoop,
The sound of something delicate shattered.

My wife stirs, Be glad, she says,
Sound doesn't carry far, that you don't hear
The whole of it, cries in the night,
Children in other cities, hurts, silences.

And she's right, I can't hear the whole of it,
Or else I hear too much and it's noise
Or I make it noise because it's too much.

So I begin homing in on something
Around me, something distinct, my wife's
Breathing, a window's rattle. Outside,
Grass is lengthening in the dark,
And sap running up the phloem of the maple,
(Do I hear it? And how the stars must be wheeling!)
And in the far room, my children's
Hearts are keeping time, for them, for us
Who have begun to listen in earnest.

The Boy Who Had Eleven Toes

It was a sign of God's bounty,
His mother had said, the fullness
Of His love spilling over.

But he was imagining himself
Slipping on wet grass, his foot
Entering the dark cave of the mower.

Life insists, his grandfather said,
It seethes into plentitude.

But he was inventing jungle rivers,
One leg casually draped over the gunnel.
He was sleeping in the deep winters
Of extremity, fireless, tent flaps
Rattling in an Arctic wind.
How easier it was to explain
Shortages, deprivations!

Always there had been the locker rooms,
The beaches, the ten dozen fingers pointing.
"Clubfoot," he had heard, "paddlewheel."
Why should he not hope to find,
Everywhere he walked, a hundred blades
And edges whirring about his shoe?

He dreamt of the lucky anonymous,
The unseen, the not-remembered.

He dreamt of the power
Of subtraction, six
Take away one take away two
Or take away six which left zero,
A heel and ball without digits.

But sometimes he dreamt of a boy
With eleven toes limping across wide fields
Under the light of a thousand stars.
Or not limping, but one foot now
Running faster for its six toes,
Touching earth and springing further
And up, lighter because heavier.
It was a dream he dared not dream too long,
A dream of something powerful and wing-like
Pulling the rest of the body with it.
It was a dream of prairies and horizons
Steeply falling away, the body opening,
The heel, suddenly, a profusion of feathers.

These Are the Gifts

for Ariel, 2½

They are her signature:
Sea shells in our boots and slippers,
Barettes under each of our pillows,
Marbles and flecks of clay
In the deep mine of our pockets.

Some we find quickly, others
Are lost to us for weeks or months,
And when we come upon them
In our daily disorder, we are struck
By her industry, this extravagance
Which secretly replenishes
Our cupboards, baskets and drawers
With gifts from the heart.

O she ranges far and wide for her riches,
Returning with tales to astonish:
Of danger spilling like a jar of coins
Over the landing and down the stairs,
Of crabs in the graveled pathway,
Alligators in the flower beds,
And Mr. McGregor in all the gardens.

But she is undaunted, risking
Life and limb to retrieve for us
What the world mislays:
Surprise! she says, as she gives
Her mother a bouquet of sticks,
Happy birthday! she croons and squeaks
And pours into my hands a cupful
Of pebbles, gum wrappers, leaves.

What can I hope for her
As she slips into my lap full of play
And laughter, squiggling her toes
While I count them, this pig, that pig,
The one who goes to market,
The one who starves,
The one who has luck,
The one who hasn't any?

May she hold on to her courage always.
May she keep filling the world up
With the sweet presence of her mischief.
May she put her trinkets
In all the right shoes.

III

Beethoven: Sonata No. 14

for Roma

You were at the piano playing the "Moonlight,"
A name Rellstab gave it when he heard
The Adagio, and remembered moonlight
Flecking the waves of Lake Lucerne.
But this was afternoon, in Boston,
The sun lighting up your apartment
Like a flare, your fingers laboring
Against a dead middle-C, and an A
Which twanged in its several pitches.
But it was Beethoven nonetheless,
Surviving the accidents of time
And circumstance, and even the unlikely name.
Outside, three floors below,
The Asian children — Vietnamese, Cambodian? —
Recently arrived like the last of so many
Witnesses, were playing among themselves,
Squealing in their small voices to the ends
Of the street. You'd said you'd seen them
In winter, the girls in sun dresses and sandals,
The boys in short-sleeved shirts, as though
Their parents knew no changes of season,
As though one abyss, for them, were like another.
It's what we'd talked about the night before:
Privation, loss: how art, for instance,
Rises out or in spite of it, Beethoven
Tuning a deaf ear to the world, giving it back
Its notion of symphony, or Austen,
Locked at Chawton into spinsterhood and illness,
Retrieving for us from the eden of romance
A truer vision: love hard-won and difficult.
Art for life's sake we'd said: ours,
If not their own. But for the moment
We were happy as you kept on playing

Into the Minuet, a flower, Liszt had called it,
Between two voids. Always that nothingness
Which gives substance its joy, its generous
Presence. I remembered, then, my father
Visiting us on Sunday afternoons
And playing the same passages, the ice
Clinking in his Scotch as he tripped his way
To the end, his fingers never wholly accurate,
And I lingering by his side, glad enough
For all his false starts, all the repeats
Which kept him with us that much longer.
Such were the terms: each note become
A benediction and an elegy as well.
And as you slid into the Presto, that final
Whirlwind, I imagined myself among them,
The children below us, crouching to their size,
With them almost in body if not spirit
And only for the sake of being there
When, for the first time, they could hear
Beethoven's music falling down to them
From a third-floor window.
What could they have remembered,
Their faces turning upward, the arms
Stilled to their sides,
As the frenetic, ascending scales exploded
Into the sforzando chords?
Some insistent image they'd kept back?
Moonlight on waves on a lake?
The darkness which makes that possible?

Gathering Hay

Vermont, 1982

Under a sky munificently blue,
We pack the last of the windrowed hay
Into bundles, fork and heave them skyward
Onto the pick-up and its unsteady pile.
Two acres in five hours. Seven loads.
By some, a half-day's work, though I'd
Dispute it. Back at the barn, we pitch
The hay up to the loft where already
A mountain of it has risen
Through our doings. Or rather, yours.
This is an art I have not mastered,
Has taken me twice the time to do
The half you've done, though I ache well
By any measure, enough to wonder
By what faith or will did the first
To settle here endure — Andersons, MacKensies,
Browns — who with scythe and pitchfork only
Heralded the winter in, survived, begat,
And made a life out of the stubborn land
They're buried in. It is a thought
I can't hold on to, a whispering here
And not quite here, before it passes.
For want of something better, I say,
"This last load killed my back,"
Thankful I lasted long enough to have
The ache I do, the sweet complaint.
But later, as we sit on your porch
Facing townward, the house behind us,
The stubbly field behind that, thick
Enough for your horse to graze on,
You say quietly, "It feels good
To have my hay in for the winter,"
Just that, though your eyes betray

What you keep to yourself and hidden.
It's the old story of time and weather,
How too much water can cure a thirst
Beyond its wants, how some this summer
Have lost their first crop to the rain,
How some will lose the second, the cut hay
Rotting and fungal in the sodden fields,
How some may lose both, the farm, themselves.
You've timed this harvest right. Had luck.
Enough to go on for another season.
Enough, at least, to make you say
Though ruin will, in time, undo us,
"It feels good." It is enough
To sit beside you
And hear you say it.

The City Garden

It is a smallish thing, and gone to seed.
Yet we shall make of it, poor as it is,
A likely spot, a quiet parenthesis
Amid the city's rumble. At our feet,
Columbine and lily will confound
The deepest grey, geraniums bloom like suns
And blue arrive where periwinkle runs
To call down heaven's colors to the ground.

And what is heaven if it can be owned?
Neither a Penshurst nor a grand Versailles,
Our garden will content a mindful eye.
The sun which flecked the spires of Babylon
Will shine as well for us, the sweet rain fall,
The April wind blow fragrance forth for love
Of neither state nor station, and above,
The public birds will warble where they will.

The Theft

Someone broke into his home and
carefully removed all of the buttons
from his 40 sport coats and vests.

— from a news story

And touched nothing else:
Not the ingots in the hollow newel,
Or the diamond in the ice-cube,
The chalice in a pot of zinnias.
He retrieved the gold brooch from a boot,
The treasury bills from the hamper,
Checked his mailbox for a likely note.
Had he found what he was looking for,
A broken vase, the silverware
Strewn like spare change on the floor,
And things, whose worth had flared irrevocably
From their very centers, gone,
He would have nodded yes, breathed easier,
Resigned to having proven to himself
The scrutable nature of our deepest wants.
But he could make of the crime no more
Than what it was: a theft of buttons,
And what agreements he had privately
Struck with the world
And its curious ways were off.
Off like his buttons. Time looped him
Once, twice, then veered into the steep
Acclivity that is the future.
If he dreamt, breathless at night
On his bed, it was always of buttons —
Gold, blue, brown ones — tumbling upward
Into the rarefied air of the unloosened.
If he spoke, it was to himself
Save for what he could disclose:
How he had stood one day at his closet

Stupefied, leaden-legged, prepared
For every eventuality but one.
And if he wished anything, it was
To be a thief, running wild
And blessed into the streets of the city,
A hundred buttons tucked and shining
Like coins, like coins,
In the folds of his clothes,
To whom nothing was sacred,
Or else everything was.

The Telephone

It has been out of order, some trouble
In the lines, small disturbances.
In the next rowhouse, the phone
Has been ringing for so long
We want to answer it, we wish
To say, Thank you for calling,
We're here, you're there,
We can live at this distance.

It is evening, the storm heavy.
My wife says, "Let's dial for weather,"
Then remembers, then forgets, tries,
And receives the news that is no news.
"Everything is happening," she says,
"Without us!" We imagine chances missed,
Spectacular offers, invitations.
We imagine the bad news getting worse,
Evacuations, conspiracies, or someone
Just now dialing our number,
Feeling, tonight, incredibly lucky,
Or those others, happily
Doing some simple thing,
Drinking tea, arranging
A spray of flowers in a vase,
Whose lives have grown
Suddenly out of our reach.

My daughter picks the receiver up,
Puts it to her ear, "Daddy," she says,
"It's raining inside." It's a steady
Crackle of static, like rain, yes,
Or wind riffling loose pages of a book,
Or something older, maybe a background

Of noise — microwaves, radiation —
Left over from the early universe.
"Let's go," I call to my wife.
"We can't," she says, "the phone is out."

And before she knows what she's said,
She closes the shutters, turns on
All the harsh lights and whirls
In a fury from room to room
Replacing books on their shelves, coats
On their hooks, leaving a miraculous
Order in her wake. "Why do I feel
Like crying?" she asks.
If the weather were warmer, we'd open
A window, open the door, open
Ourselves up to the nightly chatter
That makes the dark familiar, random.
(Cigarettes glowing like fireflies.
Beer cans. Stoops. Improvident
Gestures. Fights, caresses.)
So what do we do?

We are dancing to a ridiculous tango
By Stravinsky. Upstairs, our daughter
Is laughing through her dreams
And we remember how the world for her
Has nothing to do with *then what happens?*
We take a sweep, we take another.
The lights are turned low, as in a script,
And I am nibbling at my wife's ear.
Hello, we whisper, hello.
This is the life. We are spinning,
Shedding off years, making
Perhaps a remarkable shift.
Now the phone is ringing.
Yes, yes, we are saying cheek
To cheek, the receiver between us,
Who is it, we are saying, who is it,
Please, who is it?

"You Can't Tell One Assassin from Another"

— a random comment

They are a rumor so much of their lives
Even the camera refuses to give them credence.
But they are there, in old photographs
Of family picnics, graduations, barbecues.
Some stand too far back, their faces
Become small moons of too much light.
Some are turned in the wrong direction
Toward something outside the picture where
We shall never go. And some, slightly blurred
As though they had arisen from a long sleep
A moment before the shutter clicked,
Seem barely among us, barely returned.
Perhaps they have always been unlucky,
The lens excluding some crucial part of them,
Though they are still ready to be taken in.
Perhaps theirs is a chemistry which undoes
Film as well as victim. Or perhaps
They are simply bad studies,
Less fascinated by themselves than we are
Who scour the first batch of wire photos
For something others have missed,
A trace in the eyes or odd twist
Of mouth, some hint to assure us
We can be more clever, we can be ready.
Is it any wonder that their last revenge
Against us is themselves, image
After sharply focused image everywhere?
Say on the courthouse steps,
Or looking out from a police-car window,
Or at a jailhouse entrance, the body strangely
Manacled and under sentence, and the face
Clean and undistinguished, almost
Too common, and yes, one of ours.

Correspondence

Enclosed please find tax forms and a dinosaur.

— opening line of a letter from a friend

The tax forms will come in handy. Thank you.
The dinosaur, on the other hand, presents me,
As you must have foreseen, with special considerations.
Not that I'm ungrateful: it is always a privilege
To receive such tokens of friendship, such gifts
From what I take to be your private collection.
And what a fine example of Mesozoic fauna it is!
How deftly it moves for its bulk
Through the rubble of our dining room,
The tin heap that is our kitchen.
And how furiously social it has become,
Holding the parlor hostage, contenting itself
Both to reside in it and eat it.
Frankly, since you are keen, it is said,
On the great herbivores of the Jurassic,
I am a bit surprised at its omnivorous nature:
Last night, it devoured our Caucasian kilim,
By morning, our mantlepiece had disappeared,
And for the last hour, it has been eyeing
Something as undramatic as our philodendron.
I use "our" with some hesitation: poised
In the doorway with her valises, my wife
In a moment of absolute resolve and high art
Declared herself with a tense and terse "I go."
As if I had a choice. As if I could have said:
"We are under a spell. Our lives are not our own."
My daughter writes from Reykjavik: "It's cold.
Will stay indefinitely. Good luck and love."
The cat has been missing for three days.
I do not complain, though I admit its presence
Has redefined for me such words as "house" or "guest"

Or "fear." And what does it ask in return?
Only my belief in something more than a name
Or a pile of bones stone-cold in a museum.
Dinosaur: terrible lizard. And I am ready
To say: "Yes, it is here, yes, it exists."
And having so avowed, I worry at the consequences,
The other catastrophes the mailman might deliver —
Meteors, droughts, ice, continental shifts —
To make a lie out of its reappearance.
You see my dilemma, the risk in such matters
Of faith, a risk my neighbors, bags packed,
Trigger-fingers ready, are loath to entertain.
What can I tell you? That we have only the names
For things we have not seen? That the names
Are dangerous enough? Of course you know.
Fiction makes a truth out of some lives
And this month, I am the odd man on the block.
But please, send no more packages, and please,
Nothing inflatable. Now, as a small proof against
What some may call my liberal imagination,
Please find enclosed shreds of our philodendron.
I am sorry it isn't a dinosaur. It isn't even
Mesozoic. But if you add water, it might grow
Into something unexpected, a jungle perhaps,
Where toucan and cockatiel may caw out your days
And fireflies change forever your notion of darkness.

Movie Extras

They are always falling into crevasses,
Misstepping into wobbles of quicksand
Or marching as foot soldiers over the world's
Edge to prove some tyrannical point.

Even with animals they are unlucky,
Snake-bitten, piranha-gnawed, mauled
By abominables, and the commonest dog
Turning on them as on evil.

If disaster follows them like a cloud,
The heavens burst, and they are
Borne away clinging, poor wretches,
To none but each other,

It is always so hero and heroine
Can come stepping blithely
Over mines and springes and rubble,
Stealing our hearts, wearing our faces.

Movie after movie, day after day
They die almost out of earshot,
Just beyond our affections,
Easily, without fanfare.

Who are they these strange expendables —
Victims of spectacular meteors,
Scorpions, cars recklessly driven, wars —
That the world should love to do them in?

They pass anonymously in the street,
Lean idly in doorways. Before the knife
Plunges, the bullet hits, they say:
Do not pity us, we could be anyone.

Renovations

Things have been filling up our rooms,
The house has become too small.
We want an addition,
We want to give the cat new ground.
We want our laps free.

*

So the hired man enters our house,
And stands in the middle of the room.
He is lean, and has the lucent eyes
Of someone unlikely to do much damage.
"Where's your help?" I ask, meaning,
Where's the buzz-saw, the jack-hammer,
The seven others like him, the bulldozer,
Meaning, what are his limits?
He shows me his sledge, the forearms
Of a blacksmith, says, "These'll do."
The cat scampers upstairs.
My wife blows me a kiss
And the front door closes softly.

*

Soon he's put a hole in the plaster
And he's working to make it bigger.
Dust falls like a fine snow
Whitening his eyebrows, the hair
On his arms, the tips of his boots.
It is falling on everything —
Furniture we've left uncovered,
Rugs, baseball bats, books, guitars,
Bric-a-brac on the mantlepiece,
Old photographs, old hats.
I say something like "Bad weather,"

Though he doesn't hear me
Over the noise of his sledge bearing down,
And out of this something
Nothing comes.

*

We were going to get rid of things,
We were going to give some away.
Every spring we have told each other
This is the year
We make a break, we clear out.

*

With a grunt, he pulls
The lathing down and we inhale
The musty scent of the occult.
To the right, there's a silver
Flash of ducting, a clutter
Of wires and angulated pipes,
Thoroughfares of them,
Bared to the light of day.
"200 feet per head," he says,
"Just so much pissing and drinking."
"Sure," I say, looking
At all the hardware,
Systems of it.

*

What am I doing?
Listening to cracks and splinters.
Watching the ailanthus outside
Lean into and away from the wind.
Shuffling through papers.
Committing things to memory.

*

Now he swings the hammer up
And brings it down like a skew
Pendulum against the outside wall,
And the shards of brick are flying.
Let him feel the resistance here,
I think, let him feel the objection.
"Be careful of the window," I say,
Meaning, be careful of everything,
The drain and sewer pipes,
The joists, the ceiling, the other good walls
Taxed and mortgaged to the hilt.
"Children" I say, "small animals,"
And he lifts, he downward arcs,
He bursts through
And the light streams in.

*

Then the huge vacancy.

*

What if I tell him, Ok,
Build it up again, make it beautiful,
Put in all the cracks to remind us.
Or what if I say, *Ok!*
Now this wall, this one, this and this,
Go to it, don't hold back!

*

I don't say anything.
I pay him, and he has the look
Of someone cheated into leaving.
He fingers the money, says,
"Sure, Jack, that'll do,"

Shoulders his sledge
And carelessly walks away
Into what other lives?

*

My wife returns.
Hers is the difficult art
Of walking gracefully
Into a disaster.
She looks at the plastic sheeting
Covering the hole in the wall.
"It's dark in here," she says,
And flips the light switch on.
She sits in the chair beside me,
The cat is meowing on my lap,
Everything is settling into place.
Soon we'll have other rooms,
New enclosures, soon we'll forget
The ghost of him there in the corner
Grinning broadly, twisting
And pitching the hammer up,
Saying without guile or malice,
"We could make something happen, Jack,
We could make history here."